Praise for Daniel Wright:

"Dan Wright's writing hits like a good friend updating you on the past few years after making eye contact in a moderately crowded bar in an industrial part of town. After sharing a hug that could pancake a Volvo, he sips a cheap beer beloved by the people of that bar. He opens himself up like a prognostic fish on a cutting board tired of Heraclitus's eternal river of sewage, but never willing to quit and always willing to take that fisherman's knife and tell the world, 'Thank you but I can do it myself!'"

-RC Patterson, author of *Black Magic*

"If we didn't love America so much, we wouldn't hate America so much. That's the spirit of Dan Wright's *Love Letters from the Underground*. These poems are love letters to Americana, American dreams—some bygone, others that never existed—and a dying planet that could keep living were it not for human nature. Yet there is levity in the verse, and the book reads easy. At once a pessimistic optimist and a benevolent nihilist, Wright turns a critical yet ever-loving eye to planet and inhabitant, nation and citizen, home and self, in this maverick third full-length collection."

-Kim Vodicka, author of *The Elvis Machine*

More Praise for Daniel Wright:

"Dan Wright is not concerned with contemporary poetic conventions, he's not writing to an audience of lit mag editors, he's writing poems that speak to the people in his world. Wright takes us on the road with him, he takes us to bars, let's us listen in on his playlists of scratchy vinyl and stretched out cassette tapes. He puts us in Greyhound stations, NYC subway stations, the shotgun seat of another poet's Saturn. He takes us out to the world in the bad part of town, in the small towns invisible from the highway, lets us look at the Pacific through a Midwesterner's eyes. There is always movement and discovery and the occasional side-eye glance at the man behind the curtain who, as we all know, is there and that the bastard is a crook. All of these poems are visceral and immediate but contain dark beauty and harsh truth."

-Shawn Pavey, author of *Survival Tips for the Pending Apocalypse*

Love Letters from the Underground

Poems 2018 - 2020

Poems by Daniel W. Wright

Kansas City   Spartan Press   Missouri

Spartan Press
Kansas City, Missouri
spartanpress.com

Copyright © Daniel Wright, 2021
First Edition: 1 3 5 7 9 10 8 6 4 2
ISBN: 978-1-952411-45-8
LCCN: 2021930788

Cover image: Josh Basco
Author photo: Gabrielle Blanton
All rights reserved. No part of this publication may be reproduced or transmitted in any form or by any means, electronic or mechanical, including photocopying, recording or by info retrieval system, without prior written permission from the author.

The author wishes to acknowledge the following people and places: Jason Ryberg and everyone at Spartan Press for believing in my work. Jason Baldinger for being one of the coolest poets to share a tour with. John Dorsey for always being an inspiration. Kevin Ridgeway for being an amazing friend and one of the best poets in the Continental 48. Zaire Imani, best damn slam poet in St. Louis, for reminding me of the power of words. Clyde Always, the Bard of the Lower Haight for always welcoming me to his open mic and always with a word of encouragement. Kim Vodicka, the spokesbitch of a generation, for daring me to be more honest with myself. All the Spartan Press poets for making Kansas City so much fun. Hope to see you all at Gilhouly's next time I'm in town. First round's on me. Dunaway Books in St. Louis, White Whale Books in Pittsburgh, and Gatsby Books in Los Angeles for being some of the best places a poet can call home. Brandon Loberg, Niko Van Dyke, Anthony Buchanan and everyone at the Beat Museum for giving me a place to read and for helping make San Francisco all the more fun. Alana Harmon, my sister from another mister who I got to enjoy the first part of my 2019 tour with. Josh Basco and Gabrielle Blanton, two of the best photographers in St. Louis. The Maness Brothers, for being one of the best bands in the world and for being on the cover. Finally, to every poet at Heart of the Heartland 2019. You were all such an inspiration!

-DWW

Some poems, or early versions of them, have appeared in the following poetry journals:

365 Days: A Poetry Anthology Volume 3, Bad Jacket, Book of Matches, BUK100 Volume 2, The Dope Fiend Daily, The Rye Whiskey Review

TABLE OF CONTENTS

There's a World Going on Underground / 1

Avec amour du fleuve Mississippi / 4

Tis of Thee / 5

Roads Point the Way / 8

From a Poet's Chair / 9

That Deadhead Weed / 11

Dream on an Unknown Cliff / 12

Hell's Old Angel / 14

Dance with the Devil / 15

Whitman's Wild Great Grandchildren / 16

When the Punk Ain't Mad Anymore / 18

Heart of the Heartland / 20

Highway 70 Revisited / 22

If You Were to Ask Missouri or Illinois,
　Each State Would Say
　The Other Doesn't Know How to Drive / 23

The Lawn / 24

Scenes in a South City Bar / 26

Rainy Night in October / 28

Blood at the Alter of St. Wall Street / 29

Special Edition / 30

Troubadour / 31

61/49 / 33

Sometimes a Rock / 35

Funky Butt / 37

Fool's Gold / 38

To All People / 40

Well, Actually U.S.A. / 41

Wendy Left Neverland / 42

Man vs Machine / 44

Jazz Trip / 46

Only a Fraction / 47

The M Train / 49

On the Stage / 50

Your Generation Doesn't Know
   What Good Music Is / 51

Meet the New Boss… / 53

Buckle Down the Rumble Seat and
   Let the Radiator Boil / 54

History Lesson III / 56

Any Other Name / 57

Britney Jean / 59

No Bluebirds / 62

Third Time's the Charm / 64

What's Up, Bub / 65

Another Major Historical Event / 66

$1,000 Bet / 68

Going Home on a Greyhound Bus / 70

For Amy,
Thanks for the travel tip.

Love Letters from the Underground

There's a World Going on Underground

No one wants the crown
since the last kings fell down
Some were slain
some took matters into their own hands
but ashes, ashes
you know the rest
Nowadays everyone's driving
to be just famous enough
to get a free drink

Devil's advocates make a hell of an argument
when good friends got their backs turned
Desperate times call for desperate people
Green shirts still in the drawer
Romanticism a novel concept
Old times becoming irrelevant
but still held dear
it was the last light we had

Are you influenced by them?
Well then, I guess you're allowed
to be here
Your shirt is your allegiance
be careful what your leaders do
because the actions of strangers
can take you down with them

The boys got a new name
and it's more ridiculous than the last
no one took them serious
until the violence began
but I guess that's history for you

Political avoidance when trying to get
a good buzz
Hummers on the sidewalks
because money and endorphins
are all you got going
Date rape punk band
older than the rest of the crowd
swears it's all rumors

Gaslighting for their own good
is what was said
so someone could sleep tonight
It was so much fun
until the leeches came in
Nothing stays pure for too long

Idols fall by the wayside for fascism
Lead singers raise arms in allegiance
the rebels are outdated
so they got nothing to lose
So many want to join the party
but they were not invited
It turned out to be a bust
when the Red Death showed up

Teeth filed down to cut through
and be remembered
Life's more interesting
when you find the deep cuts
Sex positive meets negative ends
through a new coat of paint

In time you find
the best moments were smoking cigarettes outside
because you needed to hear yourself think
and you accidentally said
the right thing at the right time

Everyone leaves
when it gets too mainstream
or too old to justify to yourself
why you're there
Some may send word
down the road
to thank you for the good times

Avec amour du fleuve Mississippi

I hear the Mississippi
asking me what I'll do
with an ocean
when I barely give a river
the time of day

It says
"Come home Danny Boy.
I'll show you adventure
if you want adventure.
My banks know
what Mark Twain has seen."

"Be still," I say
"You were mighty before me
and you are mighty still."

"Peut-etr," says the River
"mais c'est ici
que tu appartiens."

I ask the River
to repeat itself

"Maybe so," says the River
"but this is where
you belong."

Tis of Thee

Across Route 66 and down Highway 61
On the 405 and up the 101
Down from Canada to Miami on I-95
Take the California Zephyr
or fly into JFK
I want to say
I love this country
like I once did
I see so much potential to love
and much potential to be grateful for
I want to believe in that potential
I want us to be that ideal
that every American has
deep in their heart
The ones that our heroes
show we can be

I cry to my country
I yearn for the good ideas on paper
that seem to be forgotten
with the passing
of every postmodern moment
I still long
to love this country
like a madness
Instead of fighting a madness
every day
with a weapon that never works

Maybe I long for a mirage
Something I thought I saw
but I can swear it was real
for a brief moment in my youth
I thought we had it
I cry to my country
to stand for
what it used to stand up for
the laws and rights
that now are just faded ink

I beg my country
to regain its long-term memory
To call out that
which we all know
is wrong
For a handshake across the aisle
to no longer be
a treasonous act
so both sides can work together
without the prerequisite need
to sharpen one's knife
just in case
To view education as a National Security
because a well-informed electorate
can only work wonders
For information to no longer
be a dirty word
so that science and math
are no longer looked upon
by anyone
as a long con

I'm sorry if I ask for too much
The human spirit just knows
how great this country
and this world
could be
And we don't have the time
we once did
My fault for constantly believing
Beliefs comes with price
There's no pity to be had
only Buddhist truth

I won't apologize for believing
I apologize to my country if it is inconvenient
but so many know what it can really be
I see its faults
and know we can do better
I see its strengths
and love it for them
I want to be here
for the long haul

Roads Point the Way

The road isn't for everyone
Some may love the idea
of the road
The romance of the road
but few can take it
for longer
than a few days
at a time

But then there are the ones
who live for the adventure
the road offers
who ready themselves
for the pitfalls
and the promises

The pretenders will always disappear
or stay in their bubbles
and I say
you do you
but don't write a check
your ass can't cash
and never open your mouth
until you know
what the shot is

From a Poet's Chair

"Don't write no Mozart masterpiece
just have fun.
Run like a madman
offend
get your ass locked up
at least once.

Flower among the weeds
Old angel at midnight
offers reprieve
Listen close
you can hear the wind
of every voice in this room
though there is only you

Too much encouragement
No reason to do anything but smile
Take everything and make it beautiful
Look out the window
The rusted metal
of a fire escape is beautiful
The smoke
coming from rooftops is beautiful
The eyes
that look up are beautiful

Never lose that wanderlust
It may annoy some
but it is who you are.
You're going to be just fine
kid."

That Deadhead Weed

Grateful Dead bear
takes off head
to say that Jerry Garcia
can kiss his ass
Asks me if I wanna get high
He's the fifth person
to ask today

Best shit
I ever smoked

Dream on an Unknown Cliff

Her face was obscured
Though I could not see her
I knew her
She looked out
towards the ocean
smiling
as I asked her to not move
for just a second

I took in the moment
as she looked as free
as any person ever would
She told me
she hadn't seen me
smile
and that I should do it
more often
I told her
I only do it
on special occasions

As I looked out
at a setting sun
I kept looking back at her
I knew I'd wake up
soon
In that moment

I wanted to tell her that I loved her
before it was too late
As I was about to say it,
she laughed and said,
"No, you don't"

When I awoke
I felt guilty
over dreaming about her
No point in breaking my own heart
again

Hell's Old Angel

Drinking Jack Daniels
with old toothless Hell's Angel
"I got some acid
that'll make ya lose you're shit," he says
"I know the people
who made Brian Wilson go nuts
and I know who kicked
Hunter Thompson's ass!"

He keeps going on
about old stories
that are modern American mythology
Don't know how much is true
and I don't really care
I keep leaning in
until he tells me
he did security at Altamont
That's when I started
to move my seat away

Dance with the Devil

She was dressed in red
with black fishnet covering
her red shirt that said
Hairy Pussies Matter
Her hair was done up
in two ponytails
made to look
like devil horns

She'd taken lipstick
and made herself look
like she had
evil eyebrows
and a Cheshire smile

"You pay $200 to be wit de Devil?" she asked.
"No thanks," I said, "I'm fine."

Whitman's Wild Great Grandchildren

(A Poem for Kevin Ridgeway)

I met my friend in person
for the first time
at the cemetery gates
The only friend I seem to have
in all of Los Angeles
and we walked up the hill
to pay our respects to a man
who
we both knew
helped us both to be more honest
in a way
society doesn't like
But society's never really thought
much of me to begin with
so fuck it

Meeting this brother in arms of the written word
felt like meeting a reflection
knowing of past agonies
that had walked parallel roads
We paid our respects to Hank,
Shared the crazy stories
that made us who we are
and gave each other space
so we could each have a private moment
with a gravestone

Just as every honest songwriter
is a child of Woody Guthrie
Blood relation be damned
Every honest poet
is descended from Bukowski
and thus
they are descended
from Walt Whitman
They say
that even in the most dysfunctional family
there is love
Well there's no family
more loving or dysfunctional
than a family of poets

When the Punk Ain't Mad Anymore

Some may say "sellout"
when they see you got a decent living
A house that isn't wrecked
by who knows how many
wandering strangers
who knew somebody
who knew somebody that you once met
at a show too long ago to remember
who vouched for you
to say you were cool
and could let them crash
for a few days
that turned into a month

Who put a hole in the wall
as a "fuck you"
to a landlord they'll never have to meet
because any authority
is automatically part of the problem

Some may say that you don't care anymore
because you don't have time
to go to shows
where a band will spend half their set
arguing over the sound
And the venue smells
like piss and regret

Or a basement too small
to hold fifty people
at one time

They don't see the rage build within
just like it used to
when you see the news
They don't see
you putting your headphones on
and blasting The Clash as loud
as they must always be heard
even if it is too loud
for your older ears
They don't stop to think
that even Patti Smith
left CBGB

Heart of the Heartland

Sun woke me up
in beautiful Missouri country
Grass dances with the wind
Breakfast with Dorsey and Baldinger
Cows in the distance
sounding pissed with each other
Gasconade River looks beautiful today
Our drive adds to the bug collection
on the windshield

Everyday darkness
watches narratives crumble
Missouri in bloom
Most outlaws aren't villains
they just have their own code
Dirt rises on gravel roads
across the way
while *Highway 61 Revisited*
and *Tupelo Honey*
blasts from a Saturn
carrying three poets
bound for Salina, Kansas

Drinking from a large bottle
of sweet tea
confused for a 40 ounce
Rich houses by the highway

show off isolation
K-10 Highway reveals beautiful lake
as I read friends
to keep me company

Hawks fly over rolling hills
and keep clear of dust devils
Tire track clouds spread thin enough
to show the curvature of the Earth
Passing the big rigs
smiling as I think
about how truckers
are the life blood of America

Highway 70 Revisited

Orange lightning
in the purple distance
of night
The distances
still look like Paradise
The beautiful plains of Kansas
lay just beyond highway barbwire
I know why they're there
I just wish for an ideal world
where they weren't

Western Kansas winds want to remind you
of the dust bowls of yesteryear
New York tries to claim
Charlie Parker and Miles Davis
but they both belong to the mid-west

I never believe anything
until the government denies it
There's more truth in coffee shops
than most of the world

If You Were to Ask Missouri or Illinois, Each State Would Say The Other Doesn't Know How to Drive

Car horn honked
as middle finger goes up
Don't drive
on the fucking highway
unless you know
how to drive on it
asshole!

Flying J
Lot lizard central
Remember stories
that Dad used to tell me
Guess they were all true

Turn from KMOX to WBBM
Talk radio never dies
though the hosts
sound like they might
at any second

The Lawn

A man will spend too many hours
thinking about the lawn
He'll get up in the wee hours
of a day off
just to cut it
trim it
and make sure
it looks pristine
if only for a week

He will chastise any child
old enough to cut it
for not doing so
Because an uncut lawn
will get you cited by the city
and neighbors one may never meet
will judge from afar
all because a lawn
looks like a mess

He will buy poisons
to kill unwanted weeds
and fertilizer to help grass grow
He'll enjoy compliments
from the other men on the block

about how nice the lawn may look
as they stand around
watching him fix a car
Such activities are the building blocks
for suburban friendships

And when the day is done
a man will survey
the front yard of his kingdom
Though nobody ever calls it that
except him
As he'll sit on a lawn chair on the porch
Hoping the mosquitoes don't get him too bad
When the sun sets,
he'll notice any imperfections he missed
and he'll take the clippers to them
hoping he got everything
just right

And then he'll rest
sitting proudly in his lawn chair
as though it were a throne
for the lawn
is finally perfect
Though only
for a week

Scenes in a South City Bar

Hunter grabs every last inch
of the writings of Rimbaud
Lowery reads high-end William Blake
given as a gift
Neil and Drew intensely debate
about "Boots of Spanish Leather"
and "One Too Many Mornings"
Musicians and poets
just two sides of the same coin
with familial bonds
made daily over decade
Non-violent platoons
ready to lay their lives down for friends

Caroline's smile rests anxieties
River Kitten laughs warm your insides
as good as any whiskey
Leather Jackal hugs feel like home
Talks of Man Ray and Baudelaire with Baxter
RC and James play pool
as friends wait to play a winner
who they know will beat them
Irene's piano has more heart
than anything else you got
Two joints and a bottle of anything
to pass upstairs
Five in the morning means
the buses are going again

A friend and a drink
can cure so much
Let straight lines never be clouded
Help is always a call or text away
Yet we're all too mid-western polite
to ever lay our burdens down
for others to see

Rainy Night in October

An old man is fidgety
as the clock strikes the new hour
Sun sets earlier
I don't mind
because I love the blanket of night
The rain comes to visit
as I hear about
fights with the past
that lead to nothing

Water runs downhill
and so does everyone's bs
But there's still the rain
Untouched before it hits the ground
I see a kid open their mouth
to catch a few drops
and laugh with their Mom
Holding their mother's hand
as they make their way
to their car

I finish my drink
and take out my umbrella
The rain is beautiful

Blood at the Alter of St. Wall Street

I wish I could say
that the title of this poem
was a bad metaphor
thought up by a sixteen-year-old
trying to be deep

But it is not
The powers that be
literally want
the elderly to die
in the name of their business

And to all of them
I say this
You go first

Special Edition

I used to be super critical
of the *Star Wars Special Editions*
and any other additional changes
George Lucas made to a trilogy
that was
in my mind
perfect

Then one day
I sent out a poem for publication
and five seconds later
I saw how I could improve it
I'm not as critical
anymore

Troubadour

(a poem for Clyde Always)

One-man band poet laureate of free life
at Height and Fillmore
Unicycle juggler
Ukulele player
He ain't no ordinary carnival barker
He is

THE BARD OF THE LOWER HEIGHT

Loves the low life
Loves the high lives
Loves jive life
Loves the bright lights
Telling tales to Melanie Bell
in the Story Salon

Living by the five
(Yes, count 'em, FIVE)
basic rules of success
to have a fun time on planet earth
  Be humble,
    be reverent,
      be inspired,
        walk with purpose,

  and

MOST IMPORTANTLY

Whatever the fuck it is
that you decide to do
try to BE HAPPY

They say he's a rabbit man
They say he knows the origin of the Gods
They say he's possessed by a spirit
that robbed the Gold Dust Trio
at the Battle of the Bite
and fixed the ponies at the 1923 Kentucky Derby
by getting everyone liquored up
on mint juleps and insisting on another round
of "My Old Kentucky Home"

Enigmatic friend to all
   A 21st century Robin Goodfellow
     A modern-day myth
        hiding in plain sight
          Another analog soul

            in a digital world

61/49

Trekking across the skull of the continent
'round the Devil's elbow
bound for New Orleans
with old blues highway roads on fire
Everything is out there
if you tune to the right frequency
Making sure to pass through
the Devil's crossroads
Getting on 61 in Memphis
and going south until we see
where souls have been sold

I imagined that when we got there
we would see a young man with a guitar
sitting at a corner on the edge of the road
I'd ask him if he was waiting for the Devil
"Uh huh," the young man would say.
"He still comes around these parts?" I'd ask.
"Sometimes," the young man would say. "In fact, y'all better get out of here.
The Devil don't come if there's crowds. He hates them."
"I can relate," I would say.

When we got there
all we saw
was a bunch of middle-aged white men
taking pictures

Next to a giant sign with three blue guitars
to make sure you know
this is
The Crossroads
Some with their guitars
and a glimmer in their eyes
that at that moment
they could almost be Clapton

My friend turned on 49
and made his way down to Mississippi Highway 1
until we hit the crossroads at Rosedale
Where MS-1 meets Highway 8
Where some say
the real crossroads are

All that was there
was a small grocery store,
a middle school,
a sign for a Piggly Wiggly
just off in the distance,
and the faint notion
that the Devil
if he ever was here
hadn't been down this way
in a long time

Sometimes a Rock

Sometimes a rock
needs to know they're not alone
Sometimes a rock
needs help getting back up
Sometimes a rock
needs a hug
Sometimes a rock
needs to hear
they're doing the right thing
for standing up
for what they believe in

Sometimes a rock
needs to step down
Sometimes a rock
needs to let a friend
fight their own battles
Sometimes a rock
needs to keep their guard up
Sometimes a rock
needs to know
it's okay to let it down

Sometimes a rock
needs a beer at four in the morning
Sometimes a rock
needs to tell a friend
when to fuck off

Sometimes a rock
needs to remember
they can crumble from a raindrop
Sometimes a rock
needs to say something pointless
because it'll make them feel better

Funky Butt

On hot summer nights
you can cut
New Orleans air with a knife
swatting mosquitoes
sometimes the size
of small birds

If you listen close
you can hear the ghost
of the true king of this town
All hail King Bolden
whom some may call Buddy
in every loud trumpet that finds its groove
In every jazz band who makes a dollar
on a cobblestone street
In every bowl of hot jambalaya
eaten to get something in your system

In the smell
and the rumble
of the end of the Mississippi
In every jazz note that don't know
what to call itself
In every myth
looking to make a name

Fool's Gold

I never really understood
until I went out on the road
how he did it.
I guess I was too far removed
even as a member
of the working poor
so that I could see
through the bullshit smile
and con-man charisma

But now, I get it
I knew he lied through his teeth
But to see the broken spirits of those
who lived in rust belt states
who were told those few precious words
they wanted to hear
for so long:

"It's gonna be just like it was!
These factories
that moved away years ago
that everyone else said
are never coming back
Guess what,
they're coming back!
Along with your self-respect
and ability to earn a living."

To see all those people
who still hold on
to that All-American
unreal hope against the odds
I now see all the blind spots
he was able
to slither his way past
Especially when the other candidate
didn't even bother
to give those people
the time of day

I saw him make those promises on TV
but I guess
since my livelihood never depended
on a factory belt
I never understood
how precious
those words could be
to some

So now, three years later
Like tired old miners after a gold rush
those who believed the lies
are only left with fool's gold
Digging their heels in
to believe that it is the real thing
because everybody wants to live a lie
but nobody wants to be a fool

To All People

All power to all people
The world ain't getting worse
it's just getting filmed
Old hippies
ask hard truths
because they've seen
all of this before

Some people still have dreams
Jobs
Peace
Freedom
Future
If Healthcare should be mandatory
so should a living wage
to afford it

Well, Actually U.S.A.

Mansplaining Uber drivers
know the best way
to
Well, Actually…

Population: Assholes

Wendy Left Neverland

(For the Memory of Jennie Bellar, 1975 – 2019)

Stuck in shock
after hearing of your sudden passing
Keeping busy with every distraction
on my phone
I just saw you a month ago
It seems like yesterday

We're all asking each other what happened
I don't know if anyone outside family knows
South City's a little greyer today
and not just because
it's mid-November
You were a Wendy
amongst Lost Girls and Lost Boys
You always knew
when to leave Neverland

I don't want to focus on the fact
that now there's one less reason
to smile in this city
but that's all I can think about
I wanted to catch up with you
but last time I saw you
I was tired
and had to deal
with unnecessary drama
at a house party

Always thought there'd be a next time

I don't want to stop writing this poem
because when this poem is over,
all that will be left is tears
Too afraid to open my mouth for same reason
though I can feel the dam ready to burst
First met at a Crazy XXX Girlfriend show
They said you were their manager
Glad our friendship
lasted longer than the band

Our talks were always calm and to the point
neither of us believed in banal small talk
though we still awkwardly engaged in such
I don't want this poem to end
and I don't want you to be gone
All that's left is frustration and sadness
And eventually
the acceptance

There's no decent ending
for a poem like this
All I can do at this point
is repeat to myself
that I wish you were here

Goodbye

Man vs Machine

John Henry may have fought
a steam-powered drill machine
but I have to face
the spellcheck
and the tiny buttons
of my touch screen phone
everyday

Tried to curse a person out
and call him a dick
though my phone was positive
I was trying to call him a duck
Half the time I try to spell "know"
it comes out "k ow"
leaving me to wonder
if I'm the only person
who has to go back
and edit social media comments
because the brain never bothers
in the heat of the moment

I feel compelled to plead my case to friends
"I know how to spell, honest!
My spellcheck keeps fucking me up!"
Down to the wire it will always be
many vs machine

I mean
man vs ma hine

...Sigh...
　GOD DAMMIT!

Man vs Machine

Fuck, I hate this thing

Jazz Trip

I wish I knew
how to tap dance worth a damn
I wish I had grace
of any sort
instead of wondering
if I'm related to Dick Van Dyke
on some level
with as often
as I trip over anything
my own words included

Only a Fraction

A woman begs forgiveness on the phone
as two friends talk about making money
The train rumbles by in beat
with a car
ready to drop its low end
with how high the bass is turned up

Clouds don't know
if they want to share rain
with the world today
So, they let loose a few embarrassed drops
before forgetting the whole thing
and letting the sun back out

Two people on the train
exchange coy glances from a distance
until a miscue ruins a love affair
that never got started
Car horn honks outside a brownstone
as an engine screams to be heard

My hipster heart falls in love
with an endless parade
of potential future ex-wives
A cavalcade of a million Annie Halls
and That Girls
who have probably fallen in love

at least once
to either the *Juno*
or *Scott Pilgrim* soundtracks
Yeah, I definitely have a type
Though I've known that
since I was thirteen
I like 'em deep, dry-humored, and literate

Jazz trios play to the benches
in Central Park
Pigeons can't get respect
as kids scare them out of the way
A woman rests her head for a moment
next to her dog
gathering her thoughts and support
from a companion more faithful
than any lover

A city of remixed George Gershwin
that will always be an old soul
A cruel bastard
who believes in tough love
It wants to see how you hang
It wants to know what you got
You can't lick your wounds for too long
It's culture incarnate
It is information
and inspiration
overload

The M Train

There's nothing
that makes me feel more
like I'm in New York
than that feeling of walking up the steps
of a subway stop
and the sensation of that first second
of hitting the street

Someone once told me
that Los Angeles is the person of your dreams
saying "Fuck me"
and New York is your worst nightmare
saying "Fuck you"
All things considered
I'll take the nightmare
It ain't so bad
when you turn the light on

On the Stage

The only difference
I've been able to find
between stand-up comics and poets
is the amount of dick jokes
told while on stage
and the fact that comedians
have a better chance
at getting paid

Your Generation Doesn't Know What Good Music Is

Yes, actually
we do
Taste is not defined
by a generation
If so,
then Baby Boomers
would have to answer
for every shitty pop act
that came through the 1970s

But as someone
who was born fifteen years
after *Abbey Road* was released,
I know who these acts are
I listen to them almost every day
They helped form my childhood
just as much
as every contemporary '90s band
did as well

So please, knock this shit off
Yes, your generation had the best music
Congrats
But we all know it
We all love it

And those who don't
are worse for it
But as you all taught us
so many times
Don't be fooled
by what you see on TV
They tend to exaggerate things
Okay, Boomer?

Meet the New Boss...

Just because
someone stopped beating you
with a wooden bat
and started beating you
with a metal one
doesn't make
the wooden bat
any better

Buckle Down the Rumble Seat and Let the Radiator Boil

Making the run to Louisville
Looking at the beautiful wilderness
of Kentucky
with Nashville in our sights
The sign for Exit 43
barely holds itself together
and the speed limit
has been blacked out
The side of the roads
are left for the remains
of rubber, steel, and glass

Old southern soul music
spreading the gospel
at 80 miles an hour
with autumn leaves
hanging over the cars
Blue exit signs
and the fast-food logos they show
become faces in a crowd
along with every truck stop and gas station
you pass by
A million golden arches
A million Days Inns
A million lives
you'll never meet
going towards their own ways
You wonder what becomes

of those who work
at the truck stops of America

The horizon is a coyote prankster
always changing it's form
Looking upon a cove in the sky
right behind a lake
The frontier changes
from the hills of abandoned mining towns
to middle America farms
with the Smoky Mountains just over yonder
and town centers that turned into strip malls

The radio dial searches
for Westerberg, Parsons, Chilton, Clark, Prine, or Zevon
maybe Townes or Lucinda or Willie or Dolly
patron saint
Cosmic American
singer-songwriter poets
Faded billboards
with pictures of Yogi Bear
promote the nearest state park
next to signs for Adult Bookstores

Following the Ohio River
until it meets the Mississippi
Metropolis looks more like Smallville
Small town America
reeks of pot
smoked by those
who dream
of getting out

History Lesson III

Mike Watt still lives
His soulmate and best friend
does not
Subverting a genre with no rules
that can always be so regimented
standing in their declaration
along with drummer George
of WE JAM ECONO

Another road accident to the state troopers
Another member of the 27 Club to the fans
A lifetime spent
filling a hole where a heart used to be
for Mike and George
Though they do not let the death of their friend
define them
in doing so, they honor their friend's memory

Though they found some success
after their friend was gone
there was not that same magic
even edfromohio
would travel miles to tell you
that you can't beat
that extra something
of those three boys from San Pedro

Any Other Name

In the '40s
I would've been called a Red
or Commie if they wanted to be confrontational
with the basis for that
being nothing more
than my being a writer
for wearing glasses
and daring to think
outside a nondescript box

In the '60s
they would have called me a hippie
Despite my being over 30
and the fact that I'm so OCD
every time I try to grow a beard
or have longer hair
it just gets annoying
Some would've called me unpatriotic
because I wouldn't have believed
in a political pissing contest
that gave so much of a generation
PTSD

In the '80s
they would've called me a Liberal
as though that's supposed to be
an insult

for pointing out how deregulation
was going to be
the downfall of this country
And for pointing out that Reaganomics
was and is
a crock of shit

Nowadays,
certain people in the community
call me ANTIFA
as though that's supposed to be
an insult
That I'm some left-wing nut
who wants to burn the whole system down
because I don't piss, bleed, or cum
red, white, and blue
every second of my life

And they base that claim
on nothing more
than my being a writer
for wearing glasses
and daring to think
outside a nondescript box

Britney Jean

We love our idols
We love them immortalized
on pictures and stamps
We point and laugh
at their trials and tribulations
because we feel
that's the exchange
in our eyes
from us making them more famous
than anyone should ever be

In real time
we only see the money paid
for the selling of a soul
bit by bit
And so, we think
they got it made
We all buy the smoke and mirrors
as they do
Never accepting anything less
than their new class
tells them to
If love were a gift
they'd throw it out
because it'd be handmade

And the dream factory
keeps pumping them out
just different enough
to not be as similar
as last time
but familiar enough
to never rock the boat

We never see the addictions
the house arrests
by greedy family members
The indecent proposals to bit players
that are overnight successes
The stalkers with nothing better to do
or the suicide attempts
Not until it's too late

We'll see the public breakdowns
that seemingly came from nowhere
We'll see the accidental overdoses
that have already lionized so many
We'll see the low hanging fruit
told by comedians
that insult and degrade
the broken and mentally ill

And we'll say they left too soon
from James to Heath
from Janis to Amy
from Valentino to Marilyn

And those who somehow survive
are tossed aside
until they die
because that's when they'll be useful again

No Bluebirds

Something tells me
you would've hated
your 100th birthday
No bars
No poems being lived
Only idiots and pretentious pricks
like me
thinking your thoughts for you
An idol
I never met

I know I wouldn't want to get a drink with you
if you were still alive
because there'd be too many others
lined up to do so
including some
who would feel entitled
to that bragging right

I'm cautious to say your name out loud
because saying it always attracts
every asshole who never bothered to create
but who loves to think
they could create
and who waste the next ten minutes
of anyone's life
talking about a novel
they'll never write
a film they'll never make

Who think the only way
to live up to your reputation
is to drink and fuck
as much as possible
They never get it right
Because they never talk
about the bluebird
in their heart
or about the beauty
of another's fire

Third Time's the Charm

Run out of road at Venice Beach
Which is the world's way of telling you
to take it easy
Beyond there lies yesterday, tomorrow,
and whatever else
strikes Eternity's fancy

Feeling ten years older than I am
hearing songs that boast
that it never rains here
Los Angeles and I just don't gel
but I still appreciate it's efforts of kindness
Opportunity walks by every corner
The ocean waves hello

The promenade lines up promises
with guitars and those trying to hustle a cd
I look at the palm trees
and the beautiful women
so many have written about
My heart aches for home
but it's hard to beat a view
like the one at Venice Beach

What's Up, Bub

(A Poem for Neil C. Luke)

I say with every ounce of sincerity
that I hope one day
to write a poem
as good as any song
you've ever written
You write America's music
A 21st century searcher
of the cosmic American way

This poem may not see the light of day
but it's not meant for the world
Only for a friend
whose songs keep me company
while I sit cramped
and starved for a calming conversation
Tonight I think you're playing Irish Corner Pub
with those Old Souls
Wish I could be there
It's pouring where I am
I wonder what it's doing in St. Louis

I learned long ago
to never take any spark in life
for granted
I'll see you soon
good sir

Another Major Historical Event

I'm tired of being generationally tied
to a major historical event
I was tired of it after Columbine
and every other shooting
attached to my age group
I had a feeling Y2K
was a bunch of bullshit
I figured that'd be it after 9/11
shedding the last patriotic tears
I had in me
I wasn't expecting Katrina or 7/7
I was proud to be a part of the election
of Barack Obama
I was glad that 2012 was another
bunch of bullshit
I feared for my life in New York
during the Boston bombings
I almost lost all hope after 2016
and now I'm counting down the days
until shelter-in-place is over
praying that people do the right thing

I'm tired of history happening in real time
Only three months into a new decade
and we're experiencing the entirety
of the 1920s
in one fail swoop

Bars are closed,
the stock market has tanked,
and we have the effectiveness
of the Coolidge presidency
but with some '70s Nixon sprinkles of paranoia
thrown in
to make it just different enough

To whom it may concern
on behalf of my generation
Please just give us time to breathe
Please let us have one day
Just one day
without us having to choose
between debt or death
We are tired
and we just want
the simple pleasure
of taking a nap
and knowing we won't
be woken up
by the sound
of shit breaking

$1,000 Bet

I had a friend
try to bet me $1000
that the President
would get re-elected
I never replied
because I don't feel
like betting on politics
when I'm scared shitless
and overly cautious
about jinxing any chance
for a nightmare to end

But still he kept wanting to bet
Raising the stakes
Making political points
at one in the morning
like a pundit
on some cable news station
because I had made a joke
on social media

I've noticed my exhales
have become more labored
as of late
I stare at the ground
more than I do at the sky
I certainly have my opinions

but at this point
I doubt they'd change anyone's mind
and I don't want to spend my days
getting overly frustrated
at those who believe
that 2+2=5

So in the middle of the night
I said goodbye
to a longtime friend
and went on with my life
No tears shed

Going Home on a Greyhound Bus

You see America
in the bus depots
The downtrodden
and temporarily impoverished millionaires
who look down at those
who accept the facts of life
Flaunting a class they will never be

Faded farmhouse windows in the sunset
Wearing love like a long-lost crown
Hearing music from across the aisle
A sleeping man's headphones blasts a beat
that's too scared to take a risk
Just loud enough to keep me
from focusing on my own slumber

Texas train calls in the distance
The rains make the land
look like northern England
with fog covering the cell towers
Georgia peach license plates pass by
Light flirtations with the woman
sitting across from me
As a woman of almost sixty
and her daughter
get into an argument
about how much the mother
makes things up
for the sake of a reaction

White arrows point a million directions
boarding and re-boarding
left to be a riddle in a hot box
Streetlights reflect the shadows
of the fallen rain
tired from their journey,
so they decided to hitch a ride
for as long as they could hang on
The post rush hour highways still stream
red and white lights
going in opposite directions

Sweet southern breezes in Texarkana
Anxieties comb over the realities
of other lifetimes
Feeling my luck running out
Getting home by the skin of my teeth
Trying to keep texts with friends
from turning into free therapy
on both ends

I'm sure Memphis would look beautiful
if I could see it in the early morning dark
Noticing as Carl's Jr
turns into Hardees
but Rally's
hasn't yet turned
into Checkers
Clouds lifted

The stars in the country
are always the most beautiful
The road makes me feel
like a Ferlinghetti poem
A poetic guerrilla engaged
in non-violent warfare
to squee-gee third eyes clean

Dawn's early light in the Bootheel
Grass becomes golden for a moment
with the only sound being
the snoring of passengers and the engine of the bus
both going in and out of sync
with each other
So close to the victory of a journey's end
I can taste it
Missouri plains will always let me know
I'm on my way home

And then
there she is
My St. Louis
It may never be
the greatest city in the world
but the people,
the buildings,
and the history
(though not without its faults)
will always make it
the greatest city
to me

The Mississippi was right
and I am here in love
willing to dance
when the cold autumn winds die down
A journey of love and a record of hope
As I go home,
a spirit whispers
"be sure to give back"

I'll do my damndest

Daniel W. Wright is an award-nominated poet and fiction writer from St. Louis, MO. He most recently wrote the foreword for *Sacred Decay: The Art of Lauren Marx* (Dark Horse, 2021) and is the author of *Brian Epstein Died for You* (Spartan Press, 2020) and *Rodeo of the Soul* (Spartan Press, 2019). His work has appeared in print journals such as *BUK100, 365 Days,* and *Gasconade Review,* as well as online journals such as *Book of Matches.*

www.ingramcontent.com/pod-product-compliance
Lightning Source LLC
Chambersburg PA
CBHW030346100526
44592CB00010B/850